BEAR LITE INN

✻

BEAR LITE INN

✻

ABRAHAM SMITH

NEW MICHIGAN PRESS
TUCSON, ARIZONA

NEW MICHIGAN PRESS
DEPT OF ENGLISH, P. O. BOX 210067
UNIVERSITY OF ARIZONA
TUCSON, AZ 85721-0067

<http://newmichiganpress.com>

Orders and queries to <nmp@thediagram.com>.

Copyright © 2020 by Abraham Smith.
All rights reserved.

ISBN 978-1-934832-77-6. FIRST PRINTING.

Design by Ander Monson.

Cover images courtesy of the author.

CONTENTS

many swept few   1
horsefly deerfly snake eyes   4
crust eye   6
eagle body entire and for free   11
nothing more   13
this shrug of broken carrots   15
now here's a little keening   18
tiny stony bits   19
aloof aloft and crofted kings and queens   20
doe bed shells still hot   25
iced morning   28
starlings prove power lines   29
walked into the world   34
therefore i believe a blue nag neighing   37
right right fill the wood stove   39
because last seen jumping   41
don't darn the holes   44
hawk closin on mouse hapless   47
let fly all   48
from two pine up   54
ma 'mong too tall weeds   56
if i might   59
mussed rut turtle beauty   61
snus swedish croup for love   64
this evening the dew sends   69
since light is everything   71

1800's north wisconsin   72

Acknowledgments   77

For and not for Patrick Michael

"I am persuaded that fossils are alive"

—Jean-Baptiste Robinet

**

many swept few
money road rage doe
hangs from the backhoe
slaughter air
a simper one

want one thing
to tie you to eternity?
as pickaxe and
doubles for cane? it's work
your ass off

works so
entire fox bladders
bead on his head
red as the stripped deer

see he is man
could eyes closed
switchback the muscles away

handles expert every cuss word
human invented
for flies pinching
little whacks of blood
from the toughs of his hands

new i know zilch
save sinew corner stare
eyes pine white ride wide
save spun by toe pull
river cold turtle shell

since i am boy
and shot at by him
in blackout mornings
anneal my hunted skull
in the purple black ball cap
of newborn flies

cuts things
piles these
squat on grass

blackberry haze
and snaps of flies
bees gnats
no-see-ums

i remember the bees
bumped the deer's small
body smaller

bees bumping bones
bees come to roost on the sugars of death   and the flies'
punctual evil wince green reptile eye riles
unmade by dogs goating
for his obscene cavalier
pinwheel tossing off of
scraps whiter and redder and
not anything so much as
this homeplate paperplate
ripped to shit

helium leg hollow never fill
come from wherever
the wind just was
nobody's dogs
babybirdhypnotized by
cuts of shy muscle
world's largest rubies
worth what we are

worth what we are

**

horsefly deerfly snake eyes

maunder
excite

candy the rain

morning lighter
fluid wampum
bear shawl
birch bark cages

waffle god iron goldenrod

shaky shifter mumble green

grandpa harold's glass eye
grandpa max's misled owl crowd

acid rivet radish tin
of chainsaw gas
to mete fake meek

pigweed
porn lore

20 gauge
ram rod asp
30-ought-6
pimpled with rust

roughness and a shine
callous and a shine

hand down that steel

braille for

in them
raspberries
when
mosquitoes

**

crust eye
constipated children
in three pair socks
whose mama
didn't have a wing
for a mouth no

and all the children
what could these skcos
be up late by the shit
for light bulb
seemed to rain
mushroom spit down
what could them
be

why socks backward ha
ha'd mama
that holly mornin
by the leanin little
pissant tree mama
face lined world
map of rivers wider
in grape jelly laughter
shaved badger mom

and all the children
stank like wild onion
all last fall harder yet and
blocky in their motions
down old snow now
on a warped toboggan
that mocks the otter chop
of a blind man hi5ing himself
in a room with seven walls

a dose of flat soda
a moldy duck on a wall
hacked block of government cheese
that ain't sun orange
and cuts like half the last
couple bucks in change

man the fields a washed up high school star
stale brag tobacco piss redwing arcing
from the tamarack
like a bloody mary
casual stated
in a stupid country cuervo pirate song

yes the fields that creek flood
so often never grow
a good go corn
of the corners
of the eyes of the blind
little to say

now the moon mouth barks
now money grows short
that tv/vcr is next in line
to get it
at least you don't have to
lead it out back
like a dog with a pistol

tv wouldn't come anyway
the tv ain't a good tv

the kids say it's good
and hold up a finger
full of gov't cheese

dad lifts his shirt at night
dad gets a good tan from it
the second wife likes
when everybody goes
to put out cigarettes
on soap opera stars

it's morning now
the sun sure is a bad egg
bed numb leg

it's morning now
and there's a line
frozen in the snow
where the tv cord
was trying
to hold on

he just couldn't make a go
if it's that 18incher
no use in talkin
cuz it's gone
gone

in his shared room
here hookworm neck kid sits
quiet as the wind
near a man
with nothing

but his kids
shy as the swamp
buck in a swarm mind you
of late gnats it's
early booming season

reaches down
balls a sock
throws it at the wall
picks it up
throws it at the wall
picks it up
throws it at the wall

until it worms
from ball
to sock again

**

eagle body entire and for free

crystal slipper
jet skin knife

the hell of a solderer
soldier's letter home

the gapmouth criminal wrapped
in nightgowns
passed between
whaledark methcars

his little shift
torn scent
limping in
cop dog noses

wrapped and fed
to the county line
he of downturned lip
rapt in white jitter curtain

the beagle's wicked yip
far now
small as money
back a mile
soft as washed hair
soft as old money bribes

salt in the trillium faces
laid soft on the lap of
the criminal's bride-to-be

old rock among napkins
body as flutter
body as spear

how to catch a cold from angels
unhook hangers and
hustle vinegar lampshades
out need cleaning windows
and sign ensign sigh

**

nothing more
beautiful
than the nulled
vetch moon

than the lit
marlboro red
thrown from
the vehicle nothing

maybe the nineteen year nun
at the county fair
her one green eye
sty free pans west through
the nodding balloons

grey squirrels
sure to circle the smolder
can't do anything
crow birds mistake it
for broken rabbit
grow meaner

turntable vinyl shatter
suffragette cerulean

the moon
the hurled ball
hurled by a man
pregnant with beer
misses everything

what's the
matter is
we flew

**

this shrug of broken carrots
thin and whole
cork and needle
neon opiate
ponds the road

these children carry carrots
like little torches
that carrot proudmouthed
by a bone thin dog
he's rat enough
not to know
the diff between
vegetable and bone

carrot puppet
arrow finger
minnow gold

bloodshot men in
crooked jeans in
cocked camo hats
bent by stopped
trucks shove
carrots into pockets
paunchy with carrots

truck on its side in its ditch
pisses a yellow mane
the crippled windshield
so many glass bits
some glass clean
afternoon friend sun
some glass red
shine share shun

believe i will rip the nose off the radio
and cook a look at the rosary on the rearview
pinch stones for mary
like a new chopped wood
cracked handle wheelbarrow
with the lard rubbed in
wheel with a patch and a bulging goose
with a light gone log frump pulp in a shaking hurry

and with mounds of carrots
slumped from the rear
and with a child climbs unsteadily
up the carrots

shirt and a jacket
thin man no shirt
jabs his finger at what
at flies over grass
soled in glass
and blood

lazy pyre flies
raisin huckster flies
slaving locket flies

one head of sweat
cuts the gopher coughs of my spine
aim and direction
of a child's
playing ball

soft wonder
it slips down
the hill bull of spine

and the sewer
neck birds do begin
begin to crochet
crotches on sky

and the carrots
in the stomachs not so
slowly ain't so pointy
showy sure of the way

**

now here's a little keening
news   vireos
pick songbirds

from the welkin
some accelerate
mid-flight

for one
merlins among
the falcon

family   or most hawks
really hover and
dive

harvesting in
two shakes the
little makes
dawn rile

**

tiny stony bits
over the counter top lip

my rag hand fish
my dice hand slips

while i sweep i am singing
white hair her black shoes

the brown smell all day soups came to

our vodka hearts
our venison chunks
crisco and cream

her rag hand rocking
cupped hand held
open waiting

for cat scraps
for church bells
that perfect shower

of sound to the last things

**

aloof aloft and crofted kings and queens
        effortless
everybody from adams to zynkowski
in a car was the shark or the sea
        when no wind shatters the car was the shark under that
                flat glass case stone

they had a car that clicked open
        meant merriment when it shut
they had a car that kept the secret with the road

we had a car that wept
        the gossipy car the tomcat static radio flamenco car
          the fallen tail pipe light the worm like the red mouth
                cop's cigarette

we had a starring car husked a hair or three from the clover
        truffling bees
        at the county highway ditch edge
        where wild strawberries one middle finger thick
        and shotgun slug swallowing contests
        kept the local water sweet and killed

        there were holes in the car
    barn cats sometimes stepped through
        to staunch the rusted breach

      blood in reverse
      barn cats sometimes stepped through
      to deliver
seven hot kittens on the floorboards

     it was an american car
it was wide as eighteen pre-world war americans
     it was long and bad on gas and the brakes spoke
        like pigs under heavy metal duress

my mother's father worked at oscar mayer
he drank it like medicine smoked sawdust cigars
      smelled like new blood hated hotdogs
    drove a tidy toyota cussed on god and men
his teeth were brown and white and black laughing at his missed
        municipal putt
    he broke or at least swayed the steeple in the sparrow's breast

if you connect the morning star to the tree and throw a rope
    over the river's single glowing sturgeon
you will gather why
    my mother married the county's best jock and buck killer
he had eyes like her dad's and the blood was not old along his
        wrists and ankle cuffs

the bad snake sound of his piss after
    another all night bender
was all we had to knead to know

    to begin again
    the prayer against the coming dent and bruise

was his fault
    that pig car
        his stepped down potato vodka tongue
    what turned the rhubarb black
        what pierced the dog's slipping ear
            what bade the cat eyes run with broken cursive lists

i was in the back seat of that car   listen
    exhaust rose and fogged my socks
i could feel the car touching
    could feel the rain water kick up and lick the cow shit
                from the bottoms of my shoes

    o benevolent derelict car
it wasn't you   i forgive   i kiss your fender
    wasn't your long roaring rasp that cost me
the chilly hand of melissa in the 7th grade

    is *that* your car?   i guess   i suppose so

jerry's auto junk yard is the blown engine finish line for ours

today a guy
    ron by name
        a hole in his bottom lip
        a too much snuff too long hole

pinches the bolt against the screw driver nose
    pulls the mirrors from the body of our car
        cinches them down on his ford falcon

he's loud   he paid four fifty a pop
he has a face that proves knives are in wind

they ain't quite right but still
a buck back buys a scratchoff

    inside every cold thing
    heat of factors of sin

in the blown engine
    field grass
newspaper from september '73
    reports of blue ribbon boys who walk around now fat
        and men

living world
living word

mice
grip
the dirt
the bald tires
rest on

weeds cattlepunch the axles
                are okay

and the faces where the mirrors were
sing it with me now

grease fire
camp fire
holy eye
shine

**

doe bed shells still hot

dog chain clothesline
wahoos and snaps at the laundry
swamp ghosts? or clouds
with nebraska breath
come down to roost? ghost
matador bed sheet wets these
ten hundred years for buck
pulses drags his bony
sapling dream under soap
and wind scintillated whites

salsa ice cream sun
roadside grass goatee
try foreign quince tryst kindling

hey hey satellite ears
how's the boot tapper go
at the buffer of our going?
racy taste solves for octane
rabbit belly for a floored pedal flare

this fizz
new hares
burst from the truce till
when deer lay down to dream
where houses leave off and the world's all in for holy irregulars
where wood ticks punctate
sienna crazy turtle rain bug

where birches
too high for canes
try mastodon rib might

sweet deer
swelled by corn ears
skitter step swear
to twice the twilit sound

try beards like bibles
weird beards like bear cubs
beards like trapdoors to trapper's lodges

tacked pelts yes glow spill

spill enough to blind enough to see
face hairs off lost log hog cowboy lumberers lost
when the river log jam changed

and the wood ran its own damn mill
and the ankle took a fetter
and the lung a shoeful
and the fish a fishful
and the current did the barbering
one beard hair then another
and it was said of the crayfish
they were the toothbrush
of the dead and it was said of the turtles
powered by eyeballs and patience
why they rode still do ride
the soft instep of time
whose surest footfall isn't

**

iced morning

mourning fornicator
fading to the silo
for a shot of booze

tobacco birds
across stainless mooring

liquidator girds

on softs that saw sauce to survive

unseeing unseen   unctuous sophist cream

no danger no eyes

we'd all one feeling
weeds in wind be

elide elide

look a next birch nicked fawn
feather face dawn

so no calf long

**

starlings prove power lines
dream fishy wallets too
or sugared surges
or tooth pull pliers knights
ride the lands to burn the strings
tied to knobs on slamming doors

pin cushion pins
poured full of solemn squeal

c'mon come on
hollow bones
pick up junk
and tithe it as a pauper hat
to the moon and back
on beggar wolves of light

they pirate stones
they knock out howdy
they jimmy tingle
from sleeping legs
green necks red heads
nursed from tomorrow

they lacquer fancy time machines
boy howdy how sky they?
on what should have been
should have could have
lockets hung on whiskered angels

gramps in his easy chair
jalapenos from a vinegar jar
and he gums them till teaspoons of sweat
wash a gleam pocket
up under his eyes   starlings
instant coffee crystals   starlings
sliver boat captains
rowing the undertows
and the maelstroms
them fine pep flecks gliding
gramps yodeling
well i declare

well now that's pretty
good pooling wings
tree rings weird knots
we're not the only dupes
riding sad sack on nostalgia
shot for shot with the sun

how hot the great depression
put it this way a toaster
in an oven on a southnorth saddle
on a wire off a wire starlings
dabble in singed leaves set free

i wonder if the place they grip is sore

neither whipping flocks
nor falling trees
ought one be fixing to
milk foxes under   eye   deed
claire the clear-eyed
cool drink of water
i was supposed to
marry in sheboygan
we strolled that grape lake
egged lip
glorious mirroring
great jeans paused she   to roll

i skipped a stone   she skipped a stone

the stones did not stay on their feet long

o me do let darken under
claire i declare you
throw my heart into
unfeel unto
catching lake maybe
silvery green

sew wind shucked leaf tongue to my
good for something song neck bone

but what if we could if we could stand
a whale of starlings
swallowed so to coal train jonah
ah starlings ticket passengers
without ticklish skin
 just me just you

two   just   zestful
poor misguided tender tendrils

first class
float bus
ride on
piano
shrapnel

florida bethesda michigan

suspended in flicker

buoyed by trying tiny black wings

**

walked into the world
wearing grandpa's skin and
learned to count
counting his wrinkles
since first bird

with the old abacus
called slap a knee
with a fuckin fallin leaf

ears born fires dying
eyes recalled by
shrugs of steam

how to say i learned to write
with shin blood ink
tugged at the teats
of graves

see those antlers?
i shot him
i was shotgun
in the white car

i have ridden
on the wheel well
of that diesel tractor

vodka vodka
o mercy vodka
grandpa grandpa
wheeling in the rot sump leaves

weird gore
heart dark
earth inn

lay down
the hairpin
fore you heart a pine

that shower that shim

common burn
cracker limb

which one ranker?
hankie breath or eye?

wakes the woods
from the grains
against a gain
in stiffness
to hankies

nil tell till you paw in numb loess

half-eyed
last night
cup skunk

means slogging
in some pure
and natural
rock fight

and love the
unmerciful
lifter of strings

and love of family
this dusky swallow bird curve
this merciful
scissoring winch
this sweetish
hectoring denizen

**

therefore i believe a blue nag neighing
at two birds unfolds
a pharmacy from mane
to lake superior

and i believe two ton tone
licks the mare's
hairs and sings
insane recollections
of chocolate boats

and i believe the cooking skillet
the gas puddle the glassy-eyed poodle
good rice cooking in jungle pots
and the lisping
bookie and the books
of prayers
enfold as one
live trap
for the preacher
bunking with the janitor
in a hutch nicknamed
fired ants for warping chintz

and bye and bye
by the tartar sauce light
of moon snip
snap   that's
the preacher trapped
sky like a beer opener
let us say sky scalps the preacher
ten times fast so

yeah old lynx
in the old flat soda songs
real sudden like
has him his hat

he's a dandy cat
in his half live beret
i wink and he kicks
glazes with his hale hips
curbstones and hydrants and velcro laces
foaming and rotten
below the bald man ansorin
while lightnin licks the black streets
to seen

**

right right fill the wood stove
same rote as sun up cereal spill

one unfeeling glove and zero
metal stove latch feel

such is habit such is a life

a whey a weight a wait on
live dark

now whip it open to a chicken
in the dark one time

bluster bust a bloody beard one time

honey buddy how in? did you
let a dead suck an egg?

you chancery of ash you snow star
pinned on sighings down of trees

habit like a habit
like a wimple white for lightning pour

you big gale pelican brow
proud down new row dirt

try
sea bird sips sledge heavy fish
till belly trumps wings

can't
cane can't zip can't clang

just this one now squawks squats
dismounts
disclaiming
nothing

**

because last seen jumping
the couch to hide
to hide glaze on an
honest sprang
deer seen me
go bear cub when he
lit out and aiming
to gun me
skunks on
wood shavings
rhubarb raw
butter eye
lacerations
mother saints ate
pledge him
eyelids kicked wood
arm veins worm itch
i ate platefuls of pine smoke
glad for corn color buy out
sister stopped biting
down below
bones blued
blood uncorked
canned champagne
floor said jesus
lost his quick count

we longed to run
the couch seat screamed
like a shoat muffled by
the machines at oscar mayer
we were loud
had to be
not to hear i drank his orange
and vodka i knew a little fire
thumb up my throat not to hear
hearts forget they were
birds in the making they were
beating to a bridge
with one way traffic
drunk wit one true dark
old man sawing
through us see no hands
eke no wee vile
and then the color in the sky lanced
the lack of color
in the stainless steel
and i'll be damned if that goose
wasn't a mother
but there was no fight in no mouth
and some body
some old dirt under the nail
wrecked sidewinder of a guy
from the cab of a truck
the thing was he rigged
his windshield wiper fluid report

say he had a degree
in cussing over tinker
to run a sneak tube
up under dash he did
what no man did leaves
the hard-on after dreams and he
held it on his lap this long
black tube he'd run up under the dash and
he lathed it tween his
lips empurpled lips
and he shot vodka
from the windshield wiper
bucket straight in his
three teeth freon
graveyard mouth
that man
skull with wings
that man
over broken exhaust
was heard to cackle at
our ragged house and
maybe it was
the tight true turn
of the harrier and
fact that every
flying is a breaking off
of certainty or
maybe he saw our
egg shell slop white

**

don't darn the holes
do beat a spoon in time
with raccoon's recycling bin sermon
don't clay hop in flophouses
do sweep dew with the red
cone cap of the capacious fool
the cape of the halloween dracula
passing from the guts
of the closet
through a hole
size of a sexy yell
passing by
human eye patch
increments
into the wall
torn by
dynamite mouth mice
willing
soft cupped beds
one human eye patch at a time

we say the wall of doom
when the dogs
do not return   return
with the swamp itch   cuts and burrs   we say
wall of doom
when suburban houses
grow dog noses   razor flanks
suitable to
eat the insides of stone
pretty on the inside and under water
that's our new team name

pretty on the inside and under water
our game ball
sniffs its immense way in
it hits it bites it builds a hive
like a mouthful of grapefruit
in a dream of orchard trees
as freakish men

eight sweet hearts easy
wag on every limb

eighty birds above
in fine frisk and trim
believe in feasting without trying

ablutions from the autocratic wind

a potlatch flung
from the wet depths
of stolen men

**

hawk closin on mouse hapless
redwing to the rescue
flung coal dynamited rock
shot ink pots
knock knock
license registration cayenne tomato
light pip pip
mighty tornado shingle whipper
pious impious imperious riotous
anarchist trash sack
over shoes off swamp to
high knock hawk off sweeter glides
in my dreams when the CEO stands to pee
eight ten aging nickel dime churls box him out
old hoops and diamonds days
old hips like chips of flint
spark fish face pinches
upon elephant inelegant if
i do so spit the mouse trumpet
zonk pray tonk pay

**

I

let fly all
your happy dabbed clay curios
at each hummocky rise
that's to keep them off sing
like a steel drum cardinal
case you've slipped into
the minus sign shark face singe
tween black bear cub and black bear sow

one running at you one white hot mother
they say no tree hugging
for black bears outhug any old tree all day

say whoop and slap at
the nose like a shark attack sock the
freak out of the front and stand

mostly dough
by the road bend
in the gentle clasp of distance
in the gentile god of my car   with eight
hundred million trilliums popping
over near darkness beginning
i am a sucker for silent oblong

woof and drop in tag alder snap
the little shit
would be timber they lumber
a little like fire

i keep drinking
my spit   keep dreaming i am
breezing through
bear musty doors
to some buttered glade
where ponies give mouth
to mouth to flowers
and a pretty ohioan or two
loom to sponge me down

2

or polar bear only bear that stalks us
as any other prey is that
snow or bad snow?

body like new fallen snow
outbid a fuck-it-all sailor
at the estate sale
for the inventor
of the lug nut

belly and thunder in the belly of the snow

3

grandpa back scratcher
good stiff stick some brown bear claws

hawk beaks tense with mercury

hey y'all did the pink fluid full of electric eel pierce your
      personal wherewithal?

if one charges
shit fuck fire
they say run down hill
for browns run down hill poor
they may very well begin to tumble
o tumbling stumbling funny bear
very like peat bog popped graveyard sod
stuffed in a walking machine

people used to wrestle bears at county fairs
people with pig between the teeth and a penchant
for whipping the small

4

now if the grandpapa grizzly
has you pinned to a lodge pole pine
if the freaking griz has your
sweet belt loops speaking french slang
to cool mountain soil
play dead
go fetal

5

the dalai lama on about
what good means
lifts his wide finger
dips it in mulberry juice dabs scripts
a berry bloody stream every eve
on your sledded way
to the tater rust scene
in the half sleep of sweet dreams
peat bog pop and peep and
linger over
your
soonish
final
end

6

those who've lived
to see new light
by dint of going fetal fake pallor
where every number is prime
tell of the bear's chill nose
truffling down ribs
tell of the hot mop bear mouth skin
swabbing the spine

o if if and when
the bear forgets
you and goes
how like god
in his jelly roll dementia
less on tiptoes   more tin pan grease
goes and leaves the quote unquote dead
for scab king coyote to
quote unquote wrench
and the whole place silent
i mean nothing
save minty conifer wind

distant dinosaur remnant barking fastidious crows

this unholy
compost smell

letting go
your fleece o
then there is
the benevolence of woods   birdsong

quiet steady
quiet stern birdsong
mother ground
may i seem a good dough arising
in ransom bow

**

from two pine up
drop and slap
my breath out hard
not to love
beautiful
brutality

in roughness is love
at least of
hunger
high drop
hard water gap tooth
lily hydra pretty
dog rough inside

body white
river grey
steel tooth spits dupe
first born

very heavy
railroad spikes driven
into chugging
thimbles of empty to fill

fish was so clean
poor sap
all smug
in her sliding window forever

bird was what the criminal knew
when the county
name was one
he hadn't the
tongue for

just biding alarm

just
wash
bird
spike

cry ice

isis

i am
born as
fuel to
whiteblack wings
again

**

ma 'mong too tall weeds

when some thing confers
and conferring telecasts
and telecasting stirs

not the pernicious tickle of
the wood tick   children

and husbands
are for pulling
those   body in a mini needle nose

crimped and gently

out

more a stiff digit
crawls her back

some thing flinging circus sawdust jackpine
some sheen of popple skinning down dowdy
ants and paints applaud
light precise exacting slop

dogs are one thing
they want love
coyotes being nobody's dog
yip like cowboy rope tricks
take a beating from the farmer
rifle and battery jiggly flashlight
square in his much hit maw
no we don't cow to no
polka dot poet juice maw
bingo chipping moon

not of this world though the wolves
wanderers loners spirited
slabs hammered down
into drifting knots of
sleek clay blue wind grey blue grey blue grey
my mine mom mother
lone and turning
the other way begins
ma and howl potential
in a 900 years stare

tossed from the tethers
of children then worry then
then hurry then happy head rush
fortune famish my
my

beard of weeds
in her work hand
to heavy her

two glass bird chirrup

greek

too am of wold and wolf and mum and this

wind to bluff this aspen's
cheeks to spurs

till white pines
blow from the laureled orator
in her right hand

now until a new tall dark

**

if i might
sense
a petering

someone looking at
moi or i at someone as tho into
a refrigerator bare

mark me then
missing to
pauper fair
sweet sweets
wanderer inn

n and o
to the
nursing home

carrots and car oil and sun sticky pocket candy
for vest
mean

bear jaw dear
love me

that's the way plant my feet
toes too small to fool with
maybe step those
haphazard in

the vhs stuck in
is of
the wind
aspen freaking

if a toe a seed

a toe a seed

a towhee landin

an aspen bending

to towhee true

**

mussed rut turtle beauty

honey wind tinged with the soapy human
and they lightning like beads
down duck back deep in
log night lay low no light

what a dream turtles
in full swim
off clocks flying

these roadside sands
those old riverside sands
maybe oceans once
the currents of
told on by many eye antediluvians
paint pallet flotsam with currants for eyes
so unloved so given
over to any little watery twirl
anachronisms after the fashion
of the salt hair cribbage gal
glowering over the dollar sweet roll

doesn't make a dither heap
until you're stuffing the trash
with the bottom of the old box
and hap upon a patch of the '50's
the mice deigned leave whole

a dollar something for a pair of dungarees?
what eat your dungarees?

corn sugar mottled bodice beauty body

and down the sand hatch
with a mess of
ping pong lotto ball eggs

let us let us spend wins like the grass snake
in the dinosaur carrying gear
of the whipped cream echoing shell hawk white

spend the shape of the deer
the deer leave when sun returns
on feathered dungarees

and where's the place in the breeze
where the impressions of all we've said remain?

and are those cupped swirls
more beautiful than the actual word? world?

it wasn't a snake it was a limpid bendy lonesome one time grass
it was the kind loaf incidental in every try
it was ping pong

ping pong

lotto

no numbers though
nor airy cage
to lift a life

it just does
they just do

overwinter in a closed pond eye
overwinter and win

**

snus swedish croup for love from heart vine to gum line
a goodly gallon of buckshot and a dicey flame and a can
of the high life and ATV's and polaris snowmobiles to shanty bars

when we've let the oiled chain chaw sufficient
so the popple comes down   thanks steel's
volition   the last fell of the day   down

chickadees titmice nuthatches jays crows
whitetails   owl pellet and bear scat
demure dance of   undone dice of snow

and pissing in woods and
shitting in woods and blowing
white hot snot on wood chips

we make love to the tree
we make love to trail
we make love to the snow

we make love to the fever shiver
epileptic saw   we make la la to the
threewheeler seat's sprung foam

and we make roses to the chit chits
of the red squirrel and we make raisin milk
to the baahaa boohoo ravens raving

reasonable decent ahaa to the sweat
on the insides of gloves   same hot
plosive seeds the mouths of

sand brown does   paper bag prunes
spill a bread to the ankles on the sledge
of the dusk   sheriff for our four-eyed hearts

stout and fancy cleaves the velvet
lord forgive him these dainty
light brown green streaks

tattooed to the chalk and papery birches
if we cuss buck it's to pray
for november's fourth of july

cheez whiz eating '20 love to wool socks
and long underwear and the number 4 and
number 3   god bless dale's ballsy feet

and wool shirts and thermal tops and
thermoses of gas station sludge and lotto tickets and
ball caps that sour of last night's poundings

hicklove   tvprettylove
riflecocklove   poachereyelove   carrionlove
raccoonporcupinelittlebeartreedlove

the one alone man large at the bar love
keeps his dip can open   lazy link to night
his used snus kissed tender in an empty

with each spit put in warming
hot cocoa mink rapture   jaeger shot
of fisher slinking through pine alone

o we make love to the supine raw
snowmobile whine   riding open
throttle forward saddle   privates

pressed to numbness   to winterbird bulge
to the tune of a junco without one
dinner mint to spare   blue balls

laid over the gas tank   and procure is
a ducking deed and acquire is a flashing
out of conrath through the littlest

slit in woods   yeah no shit love's in car-
ving your killing sleigh through no light
sumac whips staves live evil licorice

through half light low pines like
senile sadist priests praising too and so
if you show   don't fall to sleep   drop

cash money down   yes love very feral the
rubber mallet coo of cans of pabst   pickled eggs
pickled herring pickled beets and

picking fights in bars with whoever just
brushed the pocket of my jeans   waving
castrated chevy exhaust pipes   hooting eyes red as

the gut mess of the northern lights
in blue skin these days most inflaming
but most of all we come undone   just eat them raw

pretty heat lightning high heel shoe tree
buck deer antlers screwed to shed walls
screw our vodka to orange juice

with the trigger finger and screw them
that don't know   the moon is a barrel
of ranch dip i shall not want not ash not snow

got held overnight for possession of a rifle
out a truck window and a slow ride and a shining light
and brett favre as the nightlight apostle   he never

threw a ball he threw a bible of balled swan's feet
he threw a genuine alaska grown gold he threw
the scalp off the last cave bear   he threw the first

shovelful for the new well   he threw a cake
for the first day i laid eyes on you   he threw
the sandal off the super model skinnydipping

in the surf we farm our chip and dip salts from
and wash them down with one tock of brandy for true love
two squeegee brandies for going fast as wolf shins   three

for our mothers in three pair of mismatched socks
four for our father's rankling backs   five for the river
when the ice gives the whole unholy mess gives

south like a prayer spoke soft by a chiropractor
bear-faced in a red-checkered hat   horseradish breath
he knows the nine ten ways we come out of true

wood smoke's soft cast on snow's breaks can't heal
snow down in the river   sews down in the forever hold
throwback to can't deal   to fall and to runnel   fowl and fern

would love it for my woodsy tongue to tap a place
past riot steel   and to meet you there   in the road song
picked clean by baby eagles baby mink

in the chicken let of blood by the weasel
meet you there   with that white
and airy body   eerily airy   with that

one thing only   to boast as fare

**

this evening the dew sends caro knock on wood
not kerosene this bruised eye plaint eve

yard lamps shine sleets
water eye truer sheen

spat plum pits with a bit
of bewitchingly honeyed
flesh still on

semblable sidelong

nonplussed plus two

i have hank on   allow peppermint
to spice a lake in methical glen flora

long socks circle in chants to boot
and what are the pant sheds
one three five hike spike grave

i know a yearning done dun for patience   i know a pining
doled one salt crack at a time   knead one for a bobolink
so she use leg soon   soft frock lap me

when the next then alaska can bleep
that tell a mar accent

i keep

these fish-tint hours
tween dusk and
socked dark

    the bleep being take a wolf to

now hour one my great strength   now i'm clean

where i don't think to walk after shines   night

night don't ash on me now

**

since light is everything

hello lithe january

sounding
pine bough
billets

we need only
open our mouths and
rush in a sweet

unclench hands and cash
cash cash

my little prayer
to light

dear please

caustic
milk

always

**

1800's   north wisconsin   leave it to me
to work ollie fink into the leaven   he was
an ass   had eyes like blood-fat
wood ticks wrestled from the worst dog
old snuff smeared for a beard   and a stench like trash

very famous for killing wolves

killed them clean from two counties   both rusk and taylor
a lot of feed sack tied off puppy howling   that's saying something
he poisoned them   he kept the powder at home   he was a

bachelor so there was nothing stopping him

he shook bear flesh full of poison and he laid in the bushes
during the interminable coughing and he
dragged them warm
back home at dark
with the northern lights never crass on high
and there it was he tied
eight ten beautiful wolves in the glory of middle life
by their necks by the light of the moon
up to wire

little pistol shit of a cuss of a man
leaning on his shit shack
next to ten beautiful songwriters
all by the throats

promise you if i had been the moon
snapping milk bleach pictures   i would've
i wood haft said oll old pal i'd like to take a second
one of you with my rifle and lowering
my rifle into one crater or other and cocking it touched
the trigger to gravity bang   made his bangs gravy
i would have leveled him bang fuck the stories
of old world wolves stealing babies that's bull and
ollie was too   the old creek low and testy
the new dawn cool   sky worn and wormy
awfully stinky lumbermen   fat wrists swinging
norwegian ditties winging   fat wrist lard asses leveling the

white pines out of there

he clouded hearing them sawyers singing
not soothing for they grated on the ache he already had he felt
pain this is ollie follow me here   ollie in piebald britches
piebald with bear greases   suspenders built of wolf tongues
stripped stamped knocked the fool howl out of them   getting
harder to keep his oily self up he slept in suspenders   witch wart
wolf plums   he tried to rest strapped into calcified moon rungs

his tooth hurt good   so reached
for pain kill powder   took instead

gaffed

he took the wolf poison into his hands   a pair of
rough and ready hands in the wolf urine light of
halfdawn with norwegian lard asses already singing

his two bulky never pray snakehead hands that shined a little
like something fresh varnished or yanked from water or pried from
birthing matter

ollie drank the shit down with a draw of rusty creek water in the
    half life of
dawn with lumberjacks singing now plaintive now joyful birds
    writing one
sun like a drunk on a stump with nothing but unkindness left to
    churn

old oll performed a little work   i think he pulled a weed out from

the ground   he   ollie fink   solo lobo killer   took it in his head to
    lay down

               tried to   then   fell by

his plank board bed they found him cold and down

      old tough ass fink

some there were who claimed it was his buttons they were
always poison spiders   somewhere a lone baby
wolf applauds gangbusters performs a lewd jig in the dust ollie
used to spit

      only things asked us

that we don't mind the descent   and lengthen the harness some

ACKNOWLEDGMENTS

Thanks to the editors of *The American Poetry Review, Hunger Mountain, Typo, Story South, New Orleans Review, Denver Quarterly, Shankpainter, Bird Dog, Court Green, Painted Bride Quarterly, The Canary,* and *Ecotone,* where many of these poems, in very different shapes and soundscapes, first appeared.

ABRAHAM SMITH is the author of five poetry collections—*Destruction of Man* (Third Man Books, 2018); *Ashagalomancy* (Action Books, 2015); *Only Jesus Could Icefish in Summer* (Action Books, 2014); *Hank* (Action Books, 2010); and *Whim Man Mammon* (Action Books, 2007)—and one coauthored fiction collection, *Tuskaloosa Kills* (Spork Press, 2018). In 2015, he released *Hick Poetics* (Lost Roads Press), a co-edited anthology of contemporary rural American poetry and related essays. He lives in Ogden, Utah, where he is Assistant Professor of English and Co-Director of Creative Writing at Weber State University.

❋

COLOPHON

Text is set in a digital version of Jenson, designed by Robert Slimbach in 1996, and based on the work of punchcutter, printer, and publisher Nicolas Jenson. The titles here are in Futura.

❈

NEW MICHIGAN PRESS, based in Tucson, Arizona, prints poetry and prose chapbooks, especially work that transcends traditional genre. Together with DIAGRAM, NMP sponsors a yearly chapbook competition.

DIAGRAM, a journal of text, art, and schematic, is published bimonthly at THEDIAGRAM.COM. Periodic print anthologies are available from the New Michigan Press at NEWMICHIGANPRESS.COM.

www.ingramcontent.com/pod-product-compliance
Lightning Source LLC
Chambersburg PA
CBHW031455040426
42444CB00007B/1113